M N O P Q R S T U V W

L   X

K   Y

J   Z

I   A

H   B

G   C

F   D

E   E

D   F

C   G

B   H

A   I

Z   J

Y   K

X   L

W V U T S R Q P O N M

Wrigley Field

From A to Z

BARNES
&NOBLE
BOOKS
NEW YORK

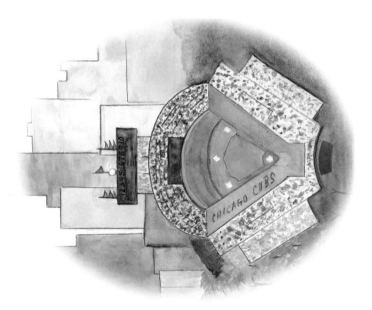

Created by the Cubs Wives for Cubs fans everywhere!

By purchasing this book you are supporting Cubs Care, official charity of the Chicago Cubs and a fund of the McCormick Tribune Foundation.

Published by Barnes & Noble Books
122 Fifth Avenue
New York, NY 10011

Text and illustrations © 2005:
Chicago National League Ball Club, Inc.
Wrigley Field, 1060 W. Addison Street, Chicago, IL 60613
www.cubs.com
773-404-CUBS

Cover illustration by Lark MacPhail

T hank you for purchasing *Wrigley Field from A to Z*. On behalf of the Cubs organization and the McCormick Tribune Foundation, I would like to thank the entire group of dedicated, enthusiastic young women who worked so hard writing and illustrating this book.

Proceeds from the book benefit Cubs Care, which supports programs such as Chicago's Children's Memorial Hospital. Cubs Care has given approximately nine million dollars to nonprofit agencies in Chicago that support youth sports programs, children with special needs, victims of domestic violence, and a variety of social service organizations that aid those in our immediate neighborhood.

Through the continued dedication of our players, coaches, and their wives, the charitable contributions of Cubs Care will be expanded to include a literacy program to aid Chicago children. This addition to our charitable giving is made possible by the proceeds we will receive from the sale of this book.

The Chicago Cubs wives are grateful for the opportunity their husbands have to play professional baseball. They appreciate the chance to work with Barnes & Noble in creating this book in order to raise funds for a charity close to their hearts, and they are pleased to be a part of this project.

As the wife of the Cubs President and CEO, Andy MacPhail, I had the privilege of working with this talented group of women. I was touched by their cooperative spirit and their determination to make an impact on the city of Chicago.

Lark MacPhail

Aa

A is for Addison Street, the address of Wrigley Field.

B

B is for the **b**leachers where our loyal fans sit in the sun and cheer.

Bb

Cc

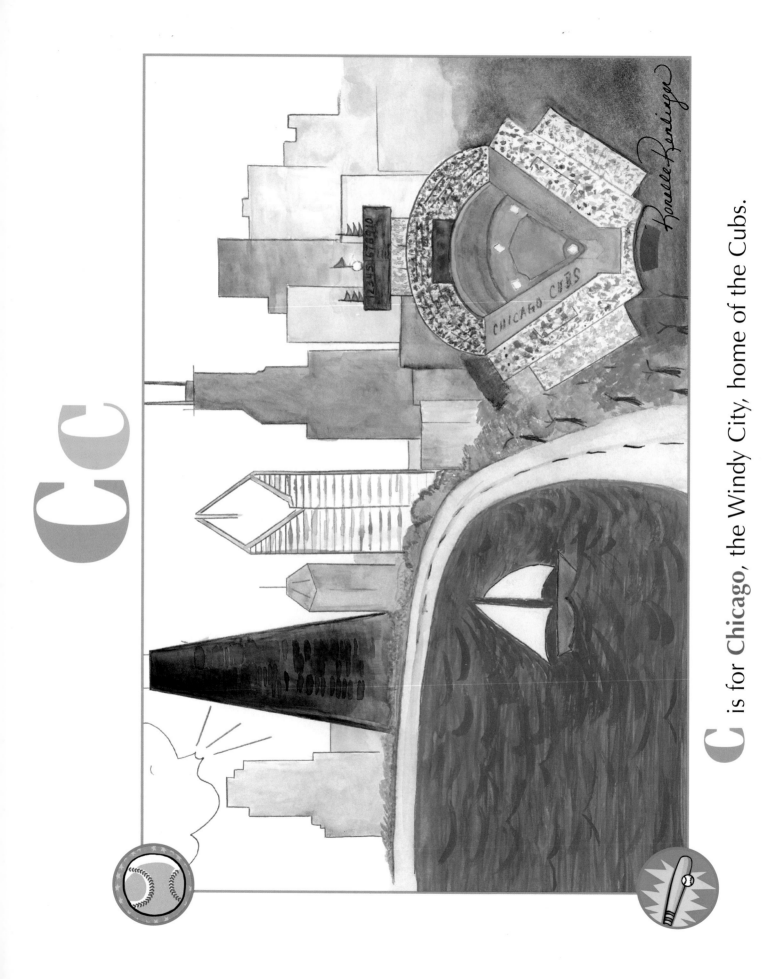

C is for **Chicago**, the Windy City, home of the Cubs.

D is for the **day games**, when the whole family can come.

Jenny Dempster

Dd

Ee

E is for the **Elevated Train** that stops at Wrigley Field.

F is for the **Friendly Confines**, our stadium's nickname.

WELCOME TO THE FRIENDLY CONFINES OF WRIGLEY FIELD

Gg

G is for the **grounds crew** who keep our field so green.

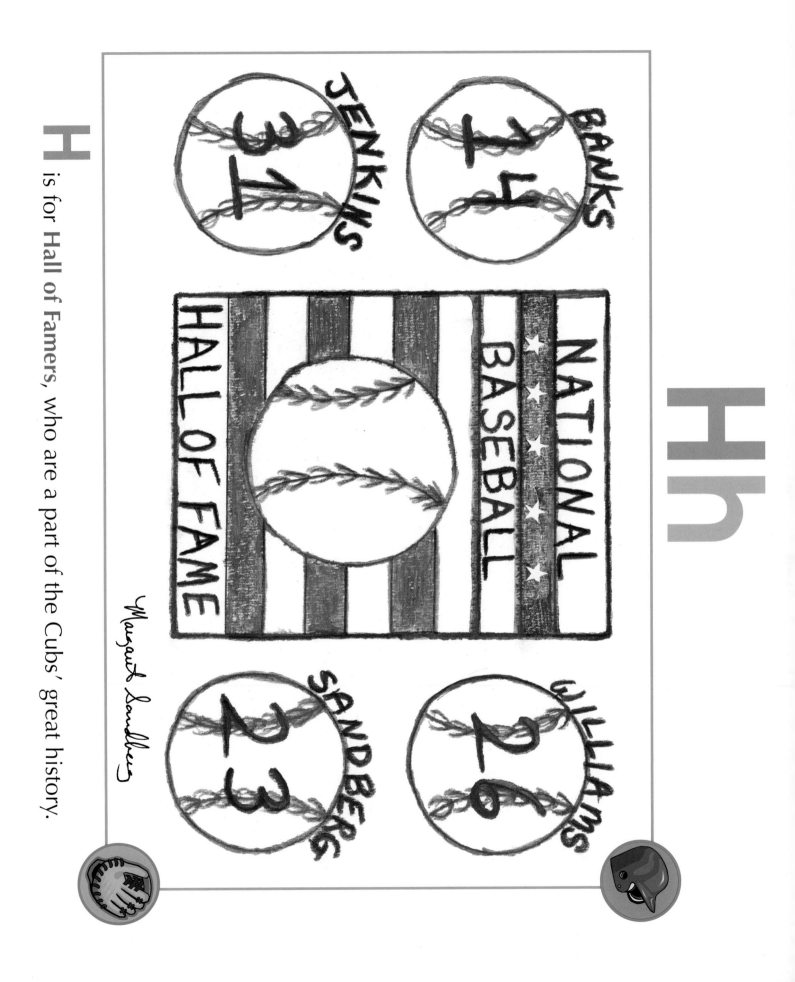

H is for Hall of Famers, who are a part of the Cubs' great history.

Hh

Ii

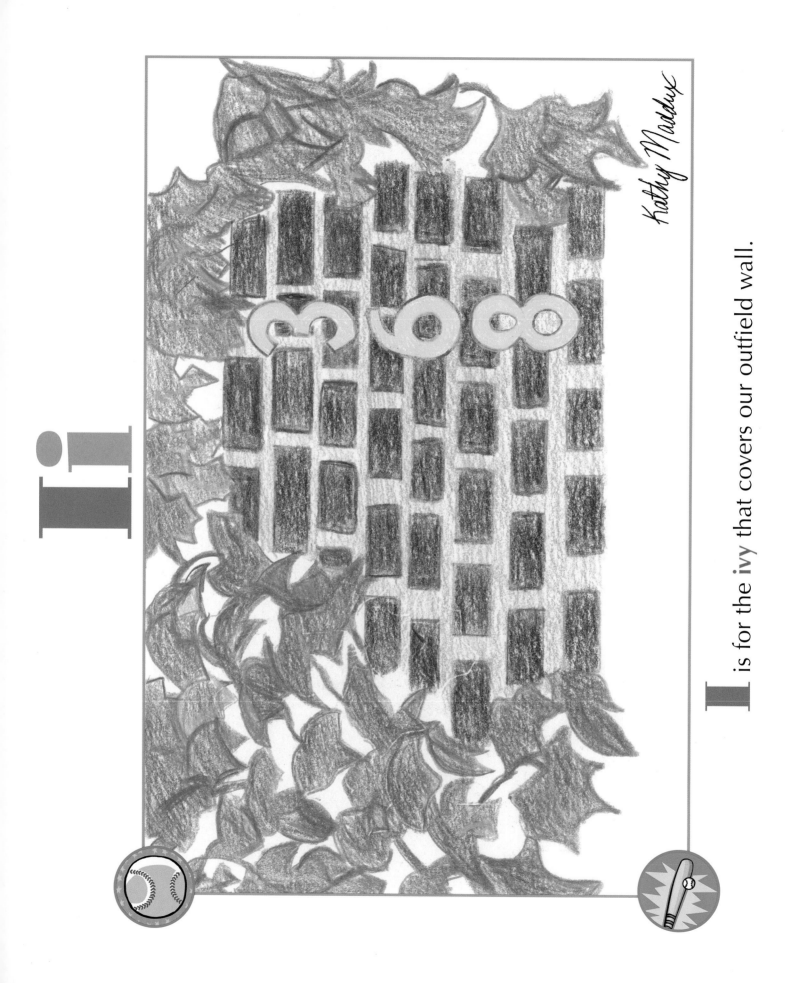

Kathy Maddux

I is for the **ivy** that covers our outfield wall.

J j

J is for jumping to make a great catch.

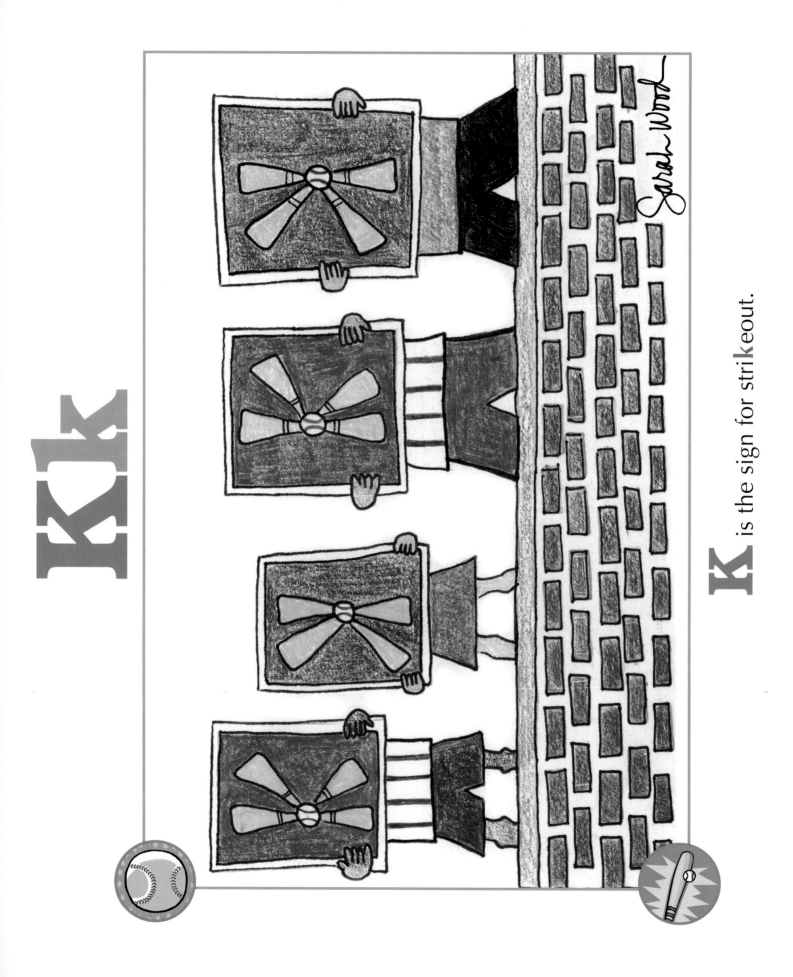

Kk

K is the sign for strikeout.

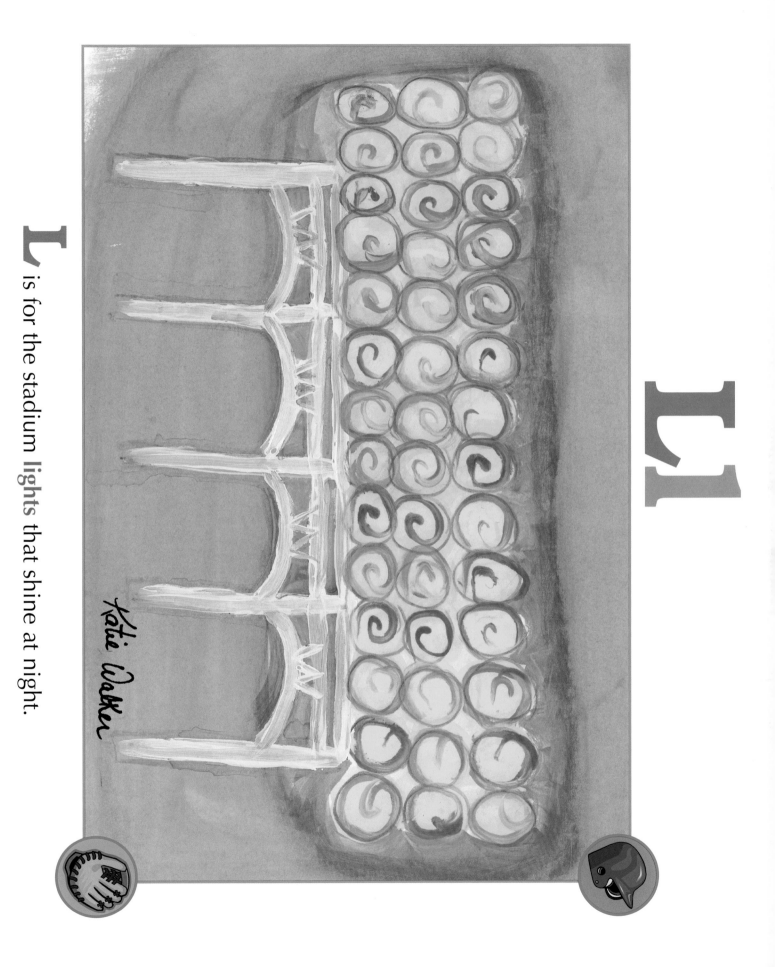

L is for the stadium **lights** that shine at night.

L l

Mm

Stephanie Barnett

M is for the **mask** that catchers wear.

N is for **North Side**, our ballpark's neighborhood, where fans cheer from the rooftops.

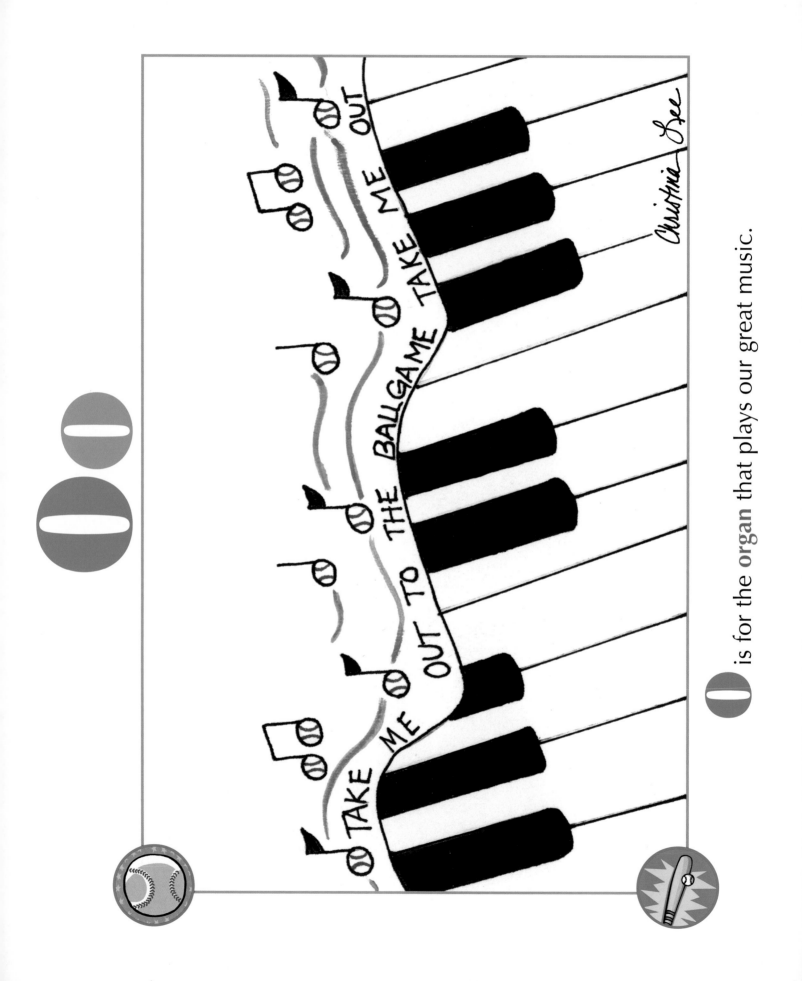

is for the **organ** that plays our great music.

P is for the pitcher on the mound.

Q is for the player running **quickly** to score.

R

R is for our famous **red sign** that welcomes everyone to Wrigley Field.

Rr

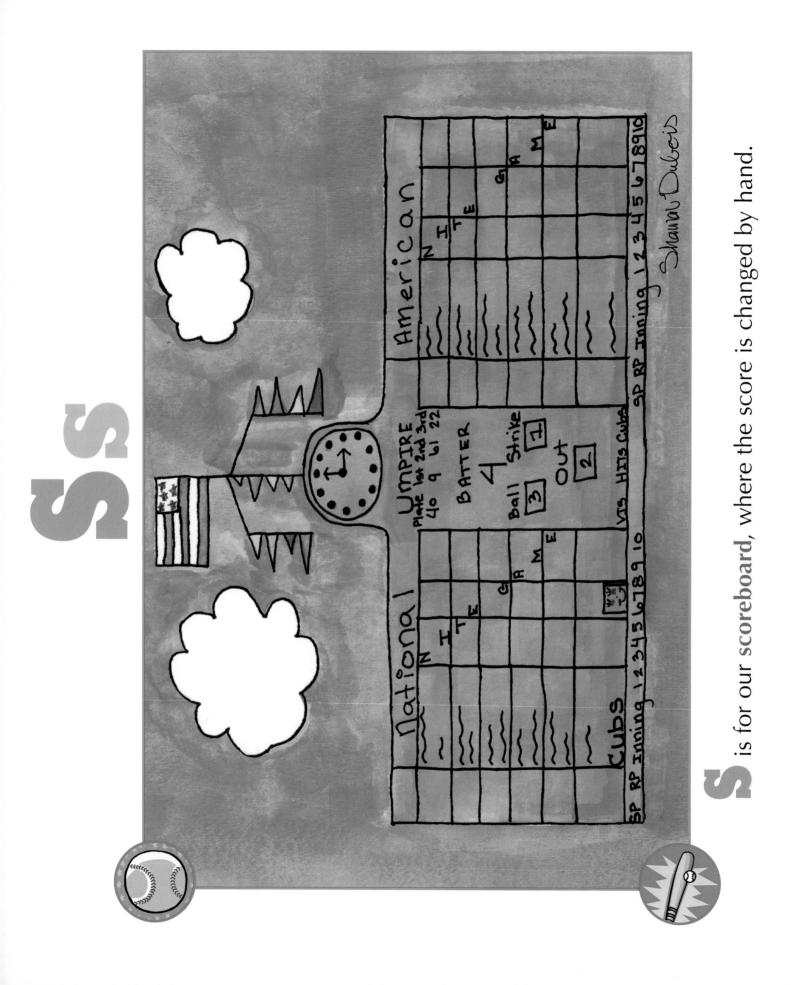

Ss

S is for our **scoreboard**, where the score is changed by hand.

T is for "Take Me Out to the Ballgame," which we sing at the 7th inning stretch.

Uu

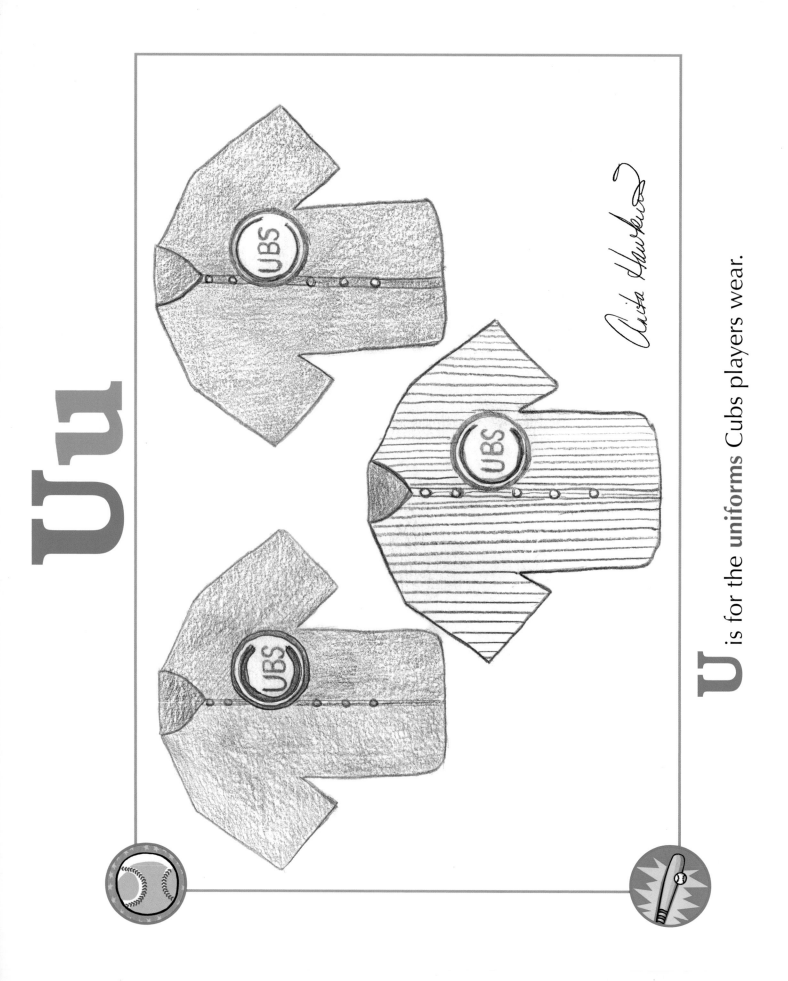

U is for the **uniforms** Cubs players wear.

V is for the vendors who sell peanuts and popcorn.

V v

Jane Rothschild

GO CUBBIES!

POPCORN

POP CORN

W is for the **win** flag that flies when we win.

X is for the extra bases a great hit gets.

Y is for yelling "Play ball!"

Z is for the strike **zone**—the place where pitchers aim.

The Chicago Cubs Players

Signed baseball photograph with numerous player autographs, including:

- #41
- Bruce Clark #2
- Billy Williams H.O.F. '87
- #13
- #37
- J.E. Jepps #59
- Sam McCann The Snage #36
- #33
- #38
- Dusty Baker #12
- Tony Stout Sr. #20
- Leon Durham 56
- Sonny Jackson #6
- Dad Pole #39
- #46
- Alex Speed #35
- #25
- Todd Hundley #28
- #22

All drawings are by Cubs Wives

A
Mia Garciaparra

B
Joanne Clines

C
Ronelle Remlinger

D
Jenny Dempster

E
Sandy Matthews

F
Tatum Borowski

G
Kristyn Burnitz

H
Margaret Sandberg

I
Kathy Maddux

J
Yudith Ramirez

K
Sarah Wood

L
Katie Walker

M
Stephanie Barrett

N
Lark MacPhail

O
Christina Lee

P
Heather Prior

Q
Marci Hollandsworth

R
Kelley Rusch

S
Shannon Dubois

T
Melissa Baker

U
Anita Hawkins

V
Jane Rothschild

W
Shirley Williams

X
Tanaha Hairston

Y
Ismary Zambrano

Z
Lydia Jenkins

The Cubs Wives thank Barbara Morgan, Publisher, and Leonard Vigliarolo, Graphic Designer, for their assistance with this book.

And a special thanks to the Cubs organization.

Printed in Canada